4th of July Recipes

by Ann Sullivan

Published in USA by:

Ann Sullivan
217 N. Seacrest Blvd #9
Boynton Beach
FL 33425

© Copyright 2017

ISBN-13: 978-1546634119
ISBN-10: 1546634118

Table of Contents

Barbequed Ribs

Ingredients

- 3 to 4 lbs. ribs, cut in pieces
- 1 c. tomato paste
- 1 tsp. salt
- 1 lg. onion
- 1/3 c. Worcestershire sauce
- 1 tsp. chili powder
- 1 1/2 c. coffee
- 2 c. water
- 1 lemon
- 1/8 tsp. liquid smoke

Instructions

In a roasting pan, add ribs with meat side up. Add lemon and onion slices over top. Roast for 30 minutes at 450 degrees. Mix together the rest of the ingredient. Boil and then pour over ribs. Lower temperature to 350 degrees. Bake for 1 hour. Baste every 15 minutes.

Russian Potato Salad

Ingredients

- 5 large potatoes
- 1 (16 ounce) package turkey hot dogs
- 5 eggs
- 5 large dill pickles, chopped
- 1 bunch green onions, chopped
- 1 (15 ounce) can baby peas, drained
- salt to taste
- 1 cup mayonnaise

Instructions

Add the potatoes to a large pot and fill with water to cover. Bring to a boil and cook 20 minutes or until tender, drain and cool. Boil eggs and hot dogs during the last ten minutes of potato boiling time and drain all then set aside to cool.

Peel potatoes and cube them. Chop up the hot dogs and combine all ingredients in a large bowl. Peel eggs and grate them over the salad. Toss each serving with mayo and salt to season

Southern Fried Chicken

Ingredients

- 1 (3 pound) whole chicken, cut into pieces
- 1 cup all-purpose flour
- salt to taste
- ground black pepper to taste
- 1 teaspoon paprika
- 1 quart vegetable oil for frying

Instructions

Season the chicken with seasonings and roll into the flour to coat.

Heat oil in a large skillet to 365 degrees F and fry chicken pieces until golden brown with cover on.

Turning only once for 15 – 20 minutes and drain on paper towels.

Dave's Coleslaw

Ingredients

- 1 head cabbage, cored and coarsely chopped
- 1 carrot, grated
- 1 sweet onion, minced
- 3 green onions, minced
- 1 dill pickle, minced
- 1 cup mayonnaise
- 2 cups buttermilk
- 2 tablespoons dill pickle juice
- 2 tablespoons vinegar
- 2 tablespoons prepared yellow mustard
- 1/2 cup white sugar
- 1 pinch cayenne pepper
- 1 teaspoon salt, divided
- 1 clove garlic

Instructions

Mix first 5 ingredients in a large bowl.

In another bowl, whisk remaining ingredients except garlic clove and mix well. Mash the salt and garlic clove and toss in dressing, pour over slaw and mix together.

Cover and chill overnight or 8 hours in refrigerator to mesh flavors together.

No Bake Cheesecake II

Ingredients

- 2 (8 ounce) packages cream cheese, softened
- 2 cups frozen whipped topping, thawed
- 1 cup white sugar
- 1 teaspoon vanilla extract
- 1 (21 ounce) can apple pie filling
- 1 (9 inch) prepared graham cracker crust

Instructions

Beat cream cheese, sugar, and the vanilla extract until it becomes a smooth mixture. Add the Cool Whip and place filling in crust and chill for 1 -2 hours before serving.

Playgroup Granola Bars

Ingredients

- 2 cups rolled oats
- 3/4 cup packed brown sugar
- 1/2 cup wheat germ
- 3/4 teaspoon ground cinnamon
- 1 cup all-purpose flour
- 3/4 cup raisins (optional)
- 3/4 teaspoon salt
- 1/2 cup honey
- 1 egg, beaten
- 1/2 cup vegetable oil
- 2 teaspoons vanilla extract

Instructions

Preheat oven to 350 degrees F and grease a 9 x 13 inch baking pan very well.

Mix the first 7 ingredients in a large bowl and make a well in the center of mixture for the egg, honey, oil, and vanilla. Using your hands, mix well and place in prepared pan, patting evenly.

Bake for 30 to 35 minutes until they start to turn a golden color on edges. Cool 5 minutes and then cut into bars while warm. Don't cool completely or they will be too hard.

Fluffy Two Step Cheesecake I

Ingredients

- 1 (8 ounce) package cream cheese
- 1/3 cup white sugar
- 1 (8 ounce) container frozen whipped topping, thawed
- 1 (9 inch) prepared graham cracker crust

Instructions

Beat cream cheese and sugar in a bowl until smooth and add the whipped topping. Add to the graham cracker crust and chill 3 hours or until set.

Grandmother's Buttermilk Cornbread

Ingredients

- 1/4 pound butter
- 2/3 cup white sugar
- 2 eggs
- 1 cup buttermilk
- 1/2 teaspoon baking soda
- 1 cup cornmeal
- 1 cup all-purpose flour
- 1/2 teaspoon salt

Instructions

Preheat oven to 375 degrees F and grease an 8" square pan.

In a large skillet, melt the butter and remove to add sugar and stir together.

Add the eggs and beat mixture until combined well.

Mix the buttermilk and baking soda and add to mixture in pan, adding remaining ingredients, stirring constantly until blended together.

Place in pan and bake for 30 to 40 minutes until toothpick tests clean.

Chili Burgers

Ingredients

- 1 1/2 pounds ground beef
- 1/2 pound Italian sausage
- 1/3 cup tomato-based chili sauce
- salt and pepper to taste

Instructions

Prepare grill for high heat and when hot, oil grate lightly.

Mix ingredients in a medium mixing bowl and shape into patties.

Cook on grill 5 minutes each side and serve with condiments of choice on buns lightly toasted.

Tex-Mex Burger with Cajun Mayo

Ingredients

- 1/2 cup mayonnaise
- 1 teaspoon Cajun seasoning
- 1 1/3 pounds ground beef sirloin
- 1 jalapeño pepper, seeded and chopped
- 1/2 cup diced white onion
- 1 clove garlic, minced
- 1 tablespoon Cajun seasoning
- 1 teaspoon Worcestershire sauce
- 4 slices pepper jack cheese
- 4 hamburger buns, split
- 4 leaves lettuce
- 4 slices tomato

Instructions

Prepare grill for medium-high heat. Mix the Cajun seasoning and mayonnaise together in a small bowl.

In another bowl mix the next 6 ingredients together well and form into balls, flattening to make patties.

Oil surface for cooking lightly and add patties to grill

cooking 5 minutes on each side. Add a slice of cheese to each before last 2 minutes and prepare buns with the Cajun mayonnaise. Top with desired condiments and enjoy.

Onion Cheese Cornbread

Ingredients

- 1 large onion, chopped
- 2 cups sour cream
- 2 eggs, beaten
- 1 (15.25 ounce) can cream-style white corn
- 1/2 teaspoon ground white pepper
- 1/2 cup unsalted butter
- 2 (8 ounce) packages white cornbread mix
- 2/3 cup buttermilk
- 1/2 teaspoon salt
- 2 cups shredded sharp Cheddar cheese

Instructions

Preheat oven to 400 degrees F and grease a 9" x 13" baking dish. In a small skillet on medium heat, melt the butter and stir in the onions to saute until tender and soft. Remove and add sour cream, set aside. Mix the cornbread mixes, eggs, buttermilk, corn, salt and pepper in a large bowl until smooth and add to the greased pan. Mix in ½ the shredded cheese into sour cream mixture and top over batter. Add the other ½ of cheese and bake for 25 – 30 minutes until firm and brown in color.

Spicy Turkey Burgers

Ingredients

- 2 pounds lean ground turkey
- 2 tablespoons minced garlic
- 1 teaspoon minced fresh ginger root
- 2 fresh green Chile peppers, diced
- 1 medium red onion, diced
- 1/2 cup fresh cilantro, finely chopped
- 1 teaspoon salt
- 1/4 cup low sodium soy sauce
- 1 tablespoon freshly ground black pepper
- 3 tablespoons paprika
- 1 tablespoon ground dry mustard
- 1 tablespoon ground cumin
- 1 dash Worcestershire sauce

Instructions

Prepare grill for high heat and when hot, lightly grease grate with oil.

Mix all ingredients in a large bowl and shape into balls, flatten into patties and place on grill for 5- 10 minutes per side until well done.

Rosemary's Burger

Ingredients

- 1 pound ground beef
- 1/2 teaspoon crushed dried rosemary
- 1 pinch salt
- 1 pinch pepper
- 1/4 teaspoon garlic powder
- 4 tablespoons butter

Instructions

Prepare grill for high heat and lightly grease with oil when hot.

Mix all ingredients in a large bowl except butter and form into patties to cook. Make a small indentation in center of each for 1 Tbs butter and mold meat around butter, then flatten into a patty. Grill for 5 – 10 minutes each side until well done.

Blueberry Sauce

Ingredients

- 2 cups fresh or frozen blueberries
- 1/4 cup water
- 1 cup orange juice
- 3/4 cup white sugar
- 1/4 cup cold water
- 3 tablespoons cornstarch
- 1/2 teaspoon almond extract
- 1/8 teaspoon ground cinnamon

Instructions

On medium heat, mix the berries with ¼ water, sugar, and orange juice, and stir slowly bringing mixture to a boil.

Mix cornstarch and ¼ cup cold water in a small bowl or cup, and slowly add mixture to berries but do not mash them.

Simmer until slightly thickened about 3 – 4 minutes. Remove and add the cinnamon and almond extract, stirring well. You may place thin sauce with water if too thick.

To Die For Blueberry Muffins

Ingredients

- 1 1/2 cups all-purpose flour
- 3/4 cup white sugar
- 1/2 teaspoon salt
- 2 teaspoons baking powder
- 1/3 cup vegetable oil
- 1 egg
- 1/3 cup milk
- 1 cup fresh blueberries
- 1/2 cup white sugar
- 1/3 cup all-purpose flour
- 1/4 cup butter, cubed
- 1 1/2 teaspoons ground cinnamon

Instructions

Preheat oven to 400 degrees F and grease muffin cups or line with muffin liners.

Mix the first 4 ingredients together in a bowl and combine. In a medium cup, add oil and egg with enough milk to fill cup and stir into flour mixture.

Mix ½ cup sugar with 1/3 cup flour,1/4 cup butter and 1 ½ tsp cinnamon to make crumb topping.

Add the blueberries, folding then into mixture and transferring all to muffin cups and topping with crumb mixture.

Bake for 20 to 25 minutes until done.

Texas Ranch Potato Salad

Ingredients

- 1 (1 ounce) package ranch dressing mix
- 2 cups mayonnaise
- 3/4 cup chopped green onion
- 1 pound bacon slices
- 5 pounds unpeeled red potatoes

Instructions

Get a large pot and fill with water, add a little salt, bring to a boil and add the potatoes cooking for 20 minutes or until tender. Drain and cool with running water then chop into cubes about 1 inch size. Place in large serving bowl and chill for 2 hours.

Add ranch dressing mix to a small bowl with mayonnaise and green onion and cover, place in refrigerator for 2 hours or so to blend.

Wrap bacon in paper towels and place on a plate, microwave for 15 minutes or so until crisp, then cool.

Add the potato mixture to the mayo mixture and crumble bacon over bowl tossing to mix in and serve.

Rico's Passionate Pink Honey Lemonade

Ingredients

- 1 cup water
- 3 fresh strawberries, sliced
- 1 cup white sugar
- 1/2 cup brown sugar
- 1 teaspoon honey

JUICE MIX

- 7 cups water
- 1 3/4 cups fresh lemon juice
- 2 slices orange

Instructions

Mix 1 cup water with remaining ingredients and bring all to a boil then reduce and simmer for 10 minutes and stir. Cool to room temperature, cover and chill in refrigerator.

Mix together water, lemon juice and orange slices in a pitcher and stir in the cooled syrup, return to chill and serve with ice.

Goat Cheese and Spinach Turkey Burgers

Ingredients

- 1 1/2 pounds ground turkey breast

- 1 cup frozen chopped spinach, thawed and drained

- 2 tablespoons goat cheese, crumbled

Instructions

Preheat broiler on the oven.

Mix the ingredients in a medium bowl and shape into patties.

Bake in the broiler for 15 minutes each side or until well done.

Corn with a Kick

Ingredients

- 1/4 cup chopped onion
- 1/4 cup chopped green pepper
- 1 tablespoon butter or margarine
- 2 cups whole kernel corn
- 1/2 medium tomato, diced
- 1 teaspoon salt
- 1/8 teaspoon pepper
- cayenne pepper to taste

Instructions

Saute' the onion and green pepper in butter in a small skillet and add the remaining ingredients then reduce heat and cover, cooking for 5 – 10 minutes or until heated through.

Angie's Dad's Best Cabbage Coleslaw

Ingredients

- 1 medium head cabbage, shredded
- 1 large red onion, diced
- 1 cup grated carrots
- 2 stalks celery, chopped
- 1 cup white sugar
- 1 cup white vinegar
- 3/4 cup vegetable oil
- 1 tablespoon salt
- 1 tablespoon dry mustard
- black pepper to taste

Instructions

Mix the first 4 ingredients in a large bowl and toss with 1 cup sugar mixing well. Add remaining ingredients to a saucepan and bring to boil. Pour the hot dressing over cabbage mix and toss well to serve.

American Potato Salad

Ingredients

- 5 pounds red potatoes
- 6 eggs
- 2 cups mayonnaise
- 1 onion, diced
- 2 green onions, thinly sliced
- 1 small green bell pepper, seeded and diced
- 3 stalks celery, thinly sliced
- 2 teaspoons salt
- 1 teaspoon ground black pepper

Instructions

Boil water in large pot and add potatoes and cook for 15 – 20 minutes until tender and firm. Drain, cool and cut into 1 inch cubes.

Cover eggs with water in a saucepan and bring to a boil then remove from heat. Cover and let set for 10 – 12 minutes in water. Take out of water and cool, then peel and chop up and place into a bowl.

Mix the potatoes and eggs in a large bowl and add mayonnaise and remaining ingredients, mixing well together, cover, and chill in refrigerator for a few hours or overnight.

Actually Delicious Turkey Burgers

Ingredients

- 3 pounds ground turkey
- 1/4 cup seasoned bread crumbs
- 1/4 cup finely diced onion
- 2 egg whites, lightly beaten
- 1/4 cup chopped fresh parsley
- 1 clove garlic, peeled and minced
- 1 teaspoon salt
- 1/4 teaspoon ground black pepper

Instructions

Place all ingredients in a large bowl and mix well hands then form into patties and cook on medium heat at 180 degrees F turning once.

Avocado Cheese Bread

Ingredients

- 2 avocados - peeled, pitted, and mashed
- 2 eggs, beaten
- 1 (8 ounce) container lemon-flavor yogurt
- 1 cup shredded Monterey Jack cheese
- 1 cup self-rising corn meal mix
- 1 tablespoon fajitas seasoning

Instructions

Preheat oven to 425 degrees F and grease a 9 x 13 inch pan.

Stir the ingredients in a large bowl until well blended and spread into the prepared pan.

Bake for 17 minutes until tests done and is golden brown.

Greek Bifteki

Ingredients

- 1 1/3 pounds ground beef

- 1 tablespoon plain yogurt

- 2 teaspoons dried thyme

- salt and pepper to taste

- 4 ounces feta cheese

Instructions

Preheat grill for indirect heat.

Mix everything except cheese in a large bowl and form into patties 2-3 inches in diameter.

Cut cheese in 4 slices and place between two patties and seal edges. Repeat with all cheese and patties and set aside.

Oil grate for grill and place bifteki on grill and cover. Cook for 15 - 20 minutes until cheese is melted through and beef is done.

Pan Seared Red Snapper

Ingredients

- 2 (4 ounce) fillets red snapper
- 1 tablespoon olive oil
- 1 lemon, juiced
- 2 tablespoons rice wine vinegar
- 1 teaspoon Dijon mustard
- 1 tablespoon honey
- 1/4 cup chopped green onions
- 1 teaspoon ground ginger

Instructions

Run snapper under cold water to rinse and pat dry. Mix the remaining ingredients in a bowl.

Heat a skillet on medium heat and coat fillets on both sides in marinade mixture, place in skillet to fry 2 – 3 minutes each side. Add the rest of mixture to skillet and simmer for 2 – 3 minutes until fish flakes easily with a fork.

Leslie's Strawberry Breakfast Chops

Ingredients

- 1/4 cup strawberry preserves
- 1 1/2 tablespoons minced garlic
- 1 tablespoon soy sauce
- 1 tablespoon prepared horseradish
- 2 pork chops
- 1 tablespoon butter
- 1 pinch cayenne pepper
- 4 fresh strawberries for garnish

Instructions

Add the preserves, garlic, soy sauce, and horseradish to a small saucepan and cook on low heat stirring until all is heated through.

Melt butter in a small skillet and add a pinch of cayenne pepper to both sides of meat, fry until browned evenly on both sides and cook on medium until done and juices run clear.

Serve with sauce poured over the chops and garnish with strawberries.

Turkey Patties

Ingredients

- 1 pound ground turkey
- 1/4 cup fine dry bread crumbs
- 1 egg
- 2 tablespoons minced green onions
- 1 clove garlic, minced
- 1 teaspoon minced fresh ginger root
- 2 tablespoons soy sauce
- 1 tablespoon vegetable oil
- 2 tablespoons chopped fresh parsley

Instructions

Blend all ingredients in a large bowl and form into patties.

Heat oil in a skillet and fry patties 2 -3 at a time for 5 minutes each side. Garnish with chopped parsley.

Boston Iced Tea

Ingredients

- 1 gallon water
- 1 cup white sugar
- 15 tea bags
- 1 (12 fluid ounce) can frozen cranberry juice concentrate

Instructions

Boil water in a large pot and add the sugar, stirring constantly add teabags and steep until you decide when its ready. Add the cranberry concentrate and cool a little while.

Iced Tea III

Ingredients

- 6 black tea bags
- 1/2 cup white sugar
- 1 gallon boiling water
- 1 (6 ounce) can frozen lemonade concentrate

Instructions

Put tea bags in a 1 gallon jar with sugar. Add boiling water. Steep for 2 hours at room temperature. Take out the tea bags, and add concentrated lemonade. Chill.

Blue Cheese Burgers

Ingredients

- 3 pounds lean ground beef
- 4 ounces blue cheese, crumbled
- 1/2 cup minced fresh chives
- 1/4 teaspoon hot pepper sauce
- 1 teaspoon Worcestershire sauce
- 1 teaspoon coarsely ground black pepper
- 1 1/2 teaspoons salt
- 1 teaspoon dry mustard
- 12 French rolls or hamburger buns

Instructions

Mix all ingredients in a large bowl and cover to refrigerate for 2 hours. Prepare grill for high heat and shape burger mixture into 12 patties to cook. Oil grill grate and cook 5 minutes each side until well done. Serve with rolls and desired condiments.

Scrumptious Strawberry Shortcake

Ingredients

- 3 cups all-purpose flour
- 1/4 cup white sugar
- 4 teaspoons baking powder
- 3/4 teaspoon cream of tartar
- 1 cup butter
- 2/3 cup heavy cream
- 1 egg, beaten
- 3 cups sliced fresh strawberries
- 3 tablespoons white sugar

Instructions

Preheat oven to 350 degrees and grease 2 baking sheets well.

MMix top 4 ingredients in a large bowl and stir in the cream with the beaten egg, cutting butter in with a pastry blender or 2 knives.

Place onto a floured surface to knead for 2 minutes, then press into half-inch thick sheet and cut into squares.

Add to baking sheets and bake for 20 minutes until

golden and sprinkle 3 Tbs sugar over sliced berries.

Let the shortcakes cool before filling with berries.

Chocolate Strawberries

Ingredients

- 5 ounces bittersweet chocolate, chopped
- 1 pint fresh strawberries with leaves

Instructions

In the top of a double boiler, melt the chocolate and stir until smooth. Dip berries in molten chocolate ¾ way to stem and place, stem side down, on a wire rack. Chill in fridge until hardened.

French Toast Stars

Ingredients

- 8 thick slices white bread
- 2 eggs
- 1/4 cup heavy cream
- 2 tablespoons honey
- 1/4 teaspoon salt
- 1/4 teaspoon ground cinnamon
- 1 tablespoon grated orange zest
- 1/2 teaspoon vanilla extract
- 3 tablespoons butter

Instructions

Add the slices of bread to a cutting board and push a star-shaped cookie cutter into the center of each and push through bread, remove the cutter and do this for all slices, putting the star-shape aside for now.

Beat the eggs in a medium bowl together with whipping cream, honey, salt, cinnamon, orange zest and vanilla extract.

Melt butter on medium heat and dip both sides of the stars in the egg mixture, then place in pan with butter and brown both sides then transfer to a warm plate while others cook.

Aloha Coleslaw

Ingredients

- 1 medium head green cabbage, rinsed and very thinly sliced

- 1 large carrot, shredded

- 1 (15 ounce) can crushed pineapple, drained

- 1 cup mayonnaise

- 1 teaspoon salt

Instructions

Mix all ingredients well together and chill for 1 hour or so before serving.

Seasoned Turkey Burgers

Ingredients

- 1 1/2 pounds ground turkey breast
- 1 (1 ounce) package dry onion soup mix
- 1/2 teaspoon ground black pepper
- 1/2 teaspoon garlic powder
- 1 1/2 tablespoons soy sauce
- 1 egg, lightly beaten (optional)
- 6 hamburger buns, split

Instructions

Place all ingredients in a large bowl and mix well hands then form into patties and cook 20 minutes on medium heat at 180 degrees F turning once. Serve with buns and desired condiments.

Potato Salad With Bacon, Olives, and Radishes

Ingredients

- 5 potatoes
- 1 pound bacon
- 2 stalks celery
- 4 small green onions
- 12 stuffed green olives
- 5 radishes
- 1/4 cup mayonnaise
- 1 tablespoon lemon juice

Instructions

Wash and peel potatoes, cutting them into ½ inch to ¾ inch pieces.

Bring a large pot of water with a dash of salt to a boil and add potatoes, cooking 10 minutes until tender but firm.

Slice bacon and wrap in paper towels to microwave for 10 – 15 minutes or cook on medium heat in skillet until brown and even.

Chop up celery, onion, olives and radishes in small pieces and place in large bowl and add the bacon and potatoes, mix well together and add remaining ingredients. Put in refrigerator to chill before serving and enjoy!

Strawberry Cake III

Ingredients

- 1 (18.25 ounce) package white cake mix
- 1 egg white
- 1 cup white sugar
- 1 cup sliced fresh strawberries

Instructions

Make cake as directed and cool on wire rack.

Beat egg whites, sugar and strawberries with electric mixer 20 minutes on high speed until stiff peaks form. Place the layer on a serving plate and put a few toothpicks in to hold it together, frosting with ¼ of the frosting. Repeat with the 2nd layer and add the 3rd layer on top, frosting the top and the sides of cake with remaining frosting.

Strawberry Cake III

Ingredients

- 1 (18.25 ounce) package white cake mix
- 1 egg white
- 1 cup white sugar
- 1 cup sliced fresh strawberries

Instructions

Make cake as directed and cool on wire rack.

Beat egg whites, sugar and strawberries with electric mixer 20 minutes on high speed until stiff peaks form.

Place the layer on a serving plate and put a few toothpicks in to hold it together, frosting with ¼ of the frosting.

Repeat with the 2nd layer and add the 3rd layer on top, frosting the top and the sides of cake with remaining frosting.

Blueberry Congealed Salad

Ingredients

- 2 (3 ounce) packages blackberry gelatin
- 2 cups boiling water
- 1 (15 ounce) can blueberries
- 1 (8 ounce) can crushed pineapple, drained with juice reserved
- 1 (8 ounce) package cream cheese, softened
- 1/2 cup white sugar
- 1 cup sour cream
- 1/2 teaspoon vanilla extract
- 1/2 cup chopped pecans

Instructions

Dissolve gelatin in the boiling water and drain the liquid from fruit cans into a measuring cup adding just enough water to make it 1 cup. Stir the juice and fruit mixtures into gelatin and transfer to the mold. Chill to firm.

Blend the cream cheese, sugar, sour cream and vanilla and add to gelatin mixture on top. Sprinkle pecans over this and chill again for 30 more minutes.

Invert bowl and serve.

Golden Sweet Cornbread

Ingredients

- 1 cup all-purpose flour
- 1 cup yellow cornmeal
- 2/3 cup white sugar
- 1 teaspoon salt
- 3 1/2 teaspoons baking powder
- 1 egg
- 1 cup milk
- 1/3 cup vegetable oil

Instructions

Preheat oven to 400 degrees F and grease a 9 inch round cake pan lightly.

Combine the remaining ingredients in a large bowl and pour into greased pan.

Bake for 20 to 25 minutes or until tests clean in the center of loaf.

Firecracker Grilled Alaska Salmon

Ingredients

- 8 (4 ounce) fillets salmon
- 1/2 cup peanut oil
- 4 tablespoons soy sauce
- 4 tablespoons balsamic vinegar
- 4 tablespoons green onions, chopped
- 3 teaspoons brown sugar
- 2 cloves garlic, minced
- 1 1/2 teaspoons ground ginger
- 2 teaspoons crushed red pepper flakes
- 1 teaspoon sesame oil
- 1/2 teaspoon salt

Instructions

Add the salmon to a glass dish and set aside. In a separate bowl, mix all other ingredients and whisk well to pour over the fish in dish. Cover and marinate in fridge for 4 – 6 hours.

Preheat grill for indirect heat and lightly oil grate. .

Grill fillets 5 inches from coals 10 minutes per inch of

thickness or until fish flakes with a fork and turn halfway through cooking.

Sweet Potato Potato Salad

Ingredients

- 2 potatoes
- 1 sweet potato
- 4 eggs
- 2 stalks celery, chopped
- 1/2 onion, chopped
- 3/4 cup mayonnaise
- 1 tablespoon prepared mustard
- 1 teaspoon salt
- 1 1/2 teaspoons ground black pepper

Instructions

Add water to a large pot and bring to a boil, add potatoes and cook 30 minutes or until firm and tender. Drain, cool, peel and chop up into 1 inch pieces.

PPlace eggs in a saucepan, cover with cold water and bring to a boil. Cover and remove to cool in water for 10 – 12 minutes. Remove from hot water and cool, peel and chop up.

In a large bowl mix the onion potatoes, celery, and eggs.

In a smaller bowl whisk remaining ingredients together and add to the potato mixture, toss well and refrigerate and serve chilled.

Ranch-Style Deviled Eggs

Ingredients

- 6 eggs
- 1/4 cup mayonnaise
- 1 teaspoon ground black pepper
- 1 teaspoon ranch dressing mix
- 1 teaspoon prepared yellow mustard
- 1 pinch paprika, for garnish (optional)

Instructions

Cover eggs with cold water in a saucepan and bring to boil, then remove from heat to cool in water for 10 – 12 minutes. Remove and cool to peel.

Cut eggs lengthwise and remove yolks to a bowl. Mash yolks with mayonnaise and mustard seasoning with pepper and ranch dressing mix and blend until smooth. Spoon into egg white halves and garnish with paprika.

Asian Beef Skewers

Ingredients

- 3 tablespoons hoisin sauce
- 3 tablespoons sherry
- 1/4 cup soy sauce
- 1 teaspoon barbecue sauce
- 2 green onions, chopped
- 2 cloves garlic, minced
- 1 tablespoon minced fresh ginger root
- 1 1/2 pounds flank steak
- skewers

Instructions

Add all ingredients to a small bowl and toss well to mix together.

Cut steak diagonally across grain into ¼ inch slices and place in a plastic bag with hoisin mixture and shake to coat well then place in fridge overnight or 2 hours.

Prepare grill for high heat and discard marinade and thread the meat on skewers.

Oil grill grate and cook skewers 3 minutes per side.

Asian Coleslaw

Ingredients

- 6 tablespoons rice wine vinegar
- 6 tablespoons vegetable oil
- 5 tablespoons creamy peanut butter
- 3 tablespoons soy sauce
- 3 tablespoons brown sugar
- 2 tablespoons minced fresh ginger root
- 1 1/2 tablespoons minced garlic
- 5 cups thinly sliced green cabbage
- 2 cups thinly sliced red cabbage
- 2 cups shredded napa cabbage
- 2 red bell peppers, thinly sliced
- 2 carrots, julienned
- 6 green onions, chopped
- 1/2 cup chopped fresh cilantro

Instructions

In a medium bowl, mix the first 7 ingredients together and whisk well.

Mix remaining ingredients in a large bowl and toss with above peanut mixture just before serving.

Restaurant-Style Coleslaw I

Ingredients

- 1 (16 ounce) package coleslaw mix
- 2 tablespoons minced onion
- 1/3 cup white sugar
- 1/2 teaspoon salt
- 1/8 teaspoon ground black pepper
- 1/4 cup milk
- 1/2 cup mayonnaise
- 1/4 cup buttermilk
- 1 1/2 tablespoons white wine vinegar
- 2 1/2 tablespoons lemon juice

Instructions

In a large bowl, mix coleslaw with onion and mix well.

Combine salt, sugar, pepper, milk, mayonnaise, buttermilk, vinegar and lemon juice and mix together until smooth. Pour the mixture over slaw and onion mixture and stir well, chill for 1 hour.

Mashed Potato Salad

Ingredients

- 5 red potatoes
- 5 Yukon Gold potatoes
- 2 tablespoons butter
- salt and pepper to taste
- 1/2 cup mayonnaise
- 1/2 cup prepared mustard
- 1/2 cup sour cream
- 1 stalk celery, finely chopped
- 1 red onion, finely diced
- 2 small sweet pickles, finely chopped
- 1 green bell pepper, chopped

Instructions

Cube and peel potatoes if you like.

Place in large saucepan and cover with water. Cook on medium heat until tender, drain and add to a large mixing bowl.

Mash the potatoes with butter and salt and pepper adding mayonnaise, mustard and sour cream mixing well. Mix in the celery, onion, pickles and green pepper and serve warm.

Mexican Bean Salad

Ingredients

- 1 (15 ounce) can black beans, rinsed and drained
- 1 (15 ounce) can kidney beans, drained
- 1 (15 ounce) can cannelloni beans, drained and rinsed
- 1 green bell pepper, chopped
- 1 red bell pepper, chopped
- 1 (10 ounce) package frozen corn kernels
- 1 red onion, chopped
- 1/2 cup olive oil
- 1/2 cup red wine vinegar
- 2 tablespoons fresh lime juice
- 1 tablespoon lemon juice
- 2 tablespoons white sugar
- 1 tablespoon salt
- 1 clove crushed garlic
- 1/4 cup chopped fresh cilantro
- 1/2 tablespoon ground cumin
- 1/2 tablespoon ground black pepper
- 1 dash hot pepper sauce
- 1/2 teaspoon chili powder

Instructions

Combine beans bell peppers, corn, and red onion in a large bowl.

In a smaller bowl, whisk olive oil, with the next 9 ingredients and season with hot sauce and chili powder.

Pour dressing over the veggies and toss to mix well. Chill thoroughly and serve cold.

Always A Winner Potato Salad

Ingredients

- 10 large baking potatoes, scrubbed
- 12 eggs
- 3 bunches green onions, chopped
- 6 dill pickles, chopped
- 1 (4 ounce) can shrimp
- 1 (4 ounce) can small shrimp, drained
- 2 cups low-fat mayonnaise
- salt and pepper to taste
- 2 tablespoons celery salt
- 2 tablespoons paprika

Instructions

Place potatoes in a large pot and cover with water, bring to a boil and remove from the water to cool.

Chop up into bite-size chunks.

Add eggs to saucepan, and cover with cold water completely. Bring to a boil for just 1 minute and cover to cool and remove. Peel and chop up into pieces.

Mix remaining ingredients together and season to taste, then chill for 2 hours and serve.

Italian-Style Deviled Eggs

Ingredients

- 12 eggs
- 1/4 cup chopped prosciutto
- 1/4 cup grated Parmesan cheese
- 1/4 cup chopped fresh chives
- 5 green olives, finely chopped
- 1/4 cup chopped red bell pepper
- 1 tablespoon Dijon mustard
- 1/2 cup sour cream
- 2 tablespoons mayonnaise
- 5 dashes hot pepper sauce, such as Frank's Red Hot
- 1/2 teaspoon garlic powder
- 1/4 teaspoon ground black pepper

Instructions

Place eggs in large pot with cold water, covering eggs with enough water, bring to a boil and remove from heat. Let stand in water for 10 -12 minutes, then remove to cool and peel.

Slice in half lengthwise and add yolks to a bowl to mash with a fork. Reserve a little Parmesan cheese and chives for garnish. Mix yolks with green olives, bell pepper, mustard, sour cream, mayonnaise, hot sauce, garlic powder, and pepper. Return yolk mix back to egg white halves and garnish with chives and Parmesan.

Steak on a Stick

Ingredients

- 1/2 cup soy sauce
- 1/4 cup olive oil
- 1/4 cup water
- 2 tablespoons molasses
- 2 teaspoons mustard powder
- 1 teaspoon ground ginger
- 1/2 teaspoon garlic powder
- 1/2 teaspoon onion powder
- 2 pounds flank steak, cut into thin strips
- 32 wooden skewers (8 inch long) soaked in water

Instructions

Combine the first 8 ingredients in a large plastic bag, seal, and shake to mix ingredients together.

Place steak strips in bag and squeeze out excess air and seal.

Chill in refrigerator at least 8 hours to marinate strips.

Preheat broiler and place meat on skewer's and add to broiling rack.

Broil the steak for 3 – 4 minutes on each side and add the meat to a serving platter.

Charbroiled Salmon

Ingredients

- 1 cup soy sauce
- 2 tablespoons red wine
- 1/2 teaspoon ground ginger
- 1/2 teaspoon ground black pepper
- 2 pounds salmon steaks
- 4 sprigs fresh parsley, for garnish
- 4 slices lemon, for garnish

Instructions

Prepare grill for medium high heat.

Combine the first 4 ingredients in a large plastic bag, seal, and shake to mix ingredients together.

Place salmon steaks in bag and squeeze out excess air and seal.

Chill in refrigerator at least 2 hours, turning frequently to keep sides in contact with liquid.

Cook 5 minutes per side basting with the extra marinade. Serve with desired garnish.

Chilly Melon Cups

Ingredients

- 1 cup water
- 1 cup sugar
- 1/2 cup lemonade concentrate
- 1/2 cup orange juice concentrate
- 4 cups watermelon balls or cubes
- 2 cups cantaloupe balls or cubes
- 2 cups cubed honeydew melon
- 2 cups pineapple chunks
- 2 cups fresh raspberries

Instructions

Mix the water, sugar, and concentrate mixes and stir until sugar is dissolved. Add the fruit and slowly stir. Place in the foil- lined or greased muffin cups and freeze.

Before serving, thaw overnight in the refrigerator or let stand at room temperature for 30 – 45 minutes until slushy.

Avocado Citrus Toss

Ingredients

- 6 cups torn salad greens
- 2 grapefruit, peeled and sectioned
- 3 navel oranges, peeled and sectioned
- 1 ripe avocado, peeled and sliced
- 1/4 cup slivered almonds, toasted

DRESSING:

- 1/2 cup vegetable oil
- 1/3 cup sugar
- 3 tablespoons vinegar
- 2 teaspoons poppy seeds
- 1 teaspoon finely chopped onion
- 1/2 teaspoon ground mustard
- 1/2 teaspoon salt

Instructions

Add all salad ingredients to a large bowl and toss well. Mix all dressing ingredients in a jar with a tight lid, and shake to combine. Pour over salad and toss to coat well.

Fresh Fruit Medley

Ingredients

- 1 medium ripe banana, sliced, divided
- 2 tablespoons mayonnaise
- 1 teaspoon sugar
- 1 kiwifruit, peeled, sliced and quartered
- 1 medium pear, cubed
- 1 small apple, cubed
- 12 seedless green grapes, halved

Instructions

Mash ½ banana slices in a large bowl and add mayonnaise and sugar and stir. Stir in the remaining ingredients and gently toss then serve.

Cucumber Potato Salad

Ingredients

- 2 medium red potatoes, cooked and cubed
- 2 tablespoons mayonnaise
- 1 tablespoon dill pickle relish
- 1 tablespoon diced pimientos
- 1/2 teaspoon celery seed
- 1/2 teaspoon dill weed
- 1/4 teaspoon salt
- 1 medium cucumber, sliced
- 2 tablespoons toasted, chopped pecans

Instructions

Mix first 7 ingredients in a bowl. Place cucumber slices on salad plates and put the salad on top.

Garnish with pecans.

Deep-Dish Blackberry Pie

Ingredients

- 3 cups fresh or frozen blackberries, thawed and drained
- 1/2 cup sugar
- 2 tablespoons cornstarch
- 1 teaspoon lemon juice
- 1/4 teaspoon ground cinnamon
- LATTICE CRUST:
- 3/4 cup all-purpose flour
- 3 teaspoons sugar, divided
- 1/4 teaspoon salt
- 3 tablespoons cold butter
- 1 tablespoon shortening
- 3 tablespoons cold water
- 1 egg white, beaten

Instructions

In a bowl, add the berries and set aside. Mix sugar and cornstarch and pour slowly over the berries in bowl. Add cinnamon and lemon juice and toss. Place in to a well-greased 1 qt baking dish.

Mix the flour, 1 tsp. sugar and salt in a bowl and cut in

the butter and the shortening till it becomes like coarse crumbs. Stir in a little water and toss with a fork. Roll out onto a floured surface and cut into strips for the latticework on top of filling and crimp the edges.

Brush with the egg whites and top with sprinkled sugar. Bake for 40 – 45 minutes until crust is a golden brown and the filling bubbles. Then cool on a wire rack.

Summertime Strawberry Punch

Ingredients

- 1 (12 fluid ounce) can frozen pink lemonade concentrate, thawed, undiluted
- 2 (10 ounce) packages frozen unsweetened strawberries, partially thawed
- 1/4 cup sugar
- 2 cups cold strong brewed tea
- 2 liters ginger ale, chilled
- ice cubes

Instructions

Mix lemonade concentrate, strawberries, and sugar in a blender. Cover and blend till smooth. Put in a pitcher or punch bowl to serve. Pour in tea and ginger ale. Add ice cubes. Serve.

Peach Cake Dessert

Ingredients

- 1 cup sugar
- 1 tablespoon all-purpose flour
- 1 teaspoon ground cinnamon
- 5 medium fresh peaches, peeled and sliced
- CAKE:
- 1/4 cup butter or margarine, softened
- 1/2 cup sugar
- 1 egg
- 1 cup all-purpose flour
- 2 teaspoons baking powder
- 1/4 teaspoon salt
- 1/4 cup milk

Instructions

Mix together sugar, flour and the cinnamon in a bowl and add the peaches to toss sugary mixture with.

Place in an 8-in greased pan and set aside. Blend the butter and sugar until creamy and beat in egg and flour baking powder and salt. Mix with creamed mixture with milk and drop over peaches in baking dish and cook for 40 - 45 minutes at 350 degrees F.

Sweet Floret Salad

Ingredients

- 1/2 cup mayonnaise
- 1/3 cup sugar
- 1/4 cup vegetable oil
- 1/4 cup vinegar
- 1 medium head cauliflower, broken into florets
- 1 3/4 pounds fresh broccoli florets
- 1 medium red onion, sliced
- 1 medium yellow bell pepper, cut into 1" pieces (optional)
- 1/2 pound sliced bacon, cooked and crumbled

Instructions

In a saucepan mix together, mayo, sugar, oil and vinegar and bring it to a boil while whisking. Cool completely and combine all other ingredients in another bowl. Pour the dressing over and toss, return to fridge to chill overnight, taking out several times to mix.

Sunny Orange Lemonade

Ingredients

- 4 1/4 cups water, divided
- 1 cup sugar
- 3/4 cup lemon juice
- 3/4 cup orange juice
- 2 teaspoons grated lemon peel
- 1 teaspoon grated orange peel
- ice cubes
- Lemon slices

Instructions

Bring 1 ¼ cups water to a boil with sugar and reduce heat to simmer for 10 minutes, cool and place in a pitcher. Add the lemon and orange juice with peels and cover to chill for 1 hour. Add the remaining water and serve over ice.

Thick 'n' Zesty Ribs

Ingredients

- 4 pounds pork baby back ribs, cut into serving size pieces
- 1 teaspoon garlic salt
- 1 cup ketchup
- 1/2 cup vinegar
- 1/4 cup sugar
- 1 1/2 teaspoons chili powder
- 1 teaspoon salt
- 1 teaspoon paprika
- 1 teaspoon ground mustard
- 1 teaspoon celery seed
- 1/2 teaspoon pepper

Instructions

Add ribs to a greased 13 x 9 x 2 inch pan and massage with garlic salt then bake for 45 minutes at 350 degrees, drain. Mix all remaining ingredients and pour mixture over ribs. Return to oven and cook for another 40 -50 minutes until tender.

Raspberry Meringue Pie

Ingredients

- 1 cup all-purpose flour
- 1/3 cup sugar
- 1 teaspoon baking powder
- 1/4 teaspoon salt
- 2 tablespoons cold butter or margarine
- 1 egg, beaten
- 2 tablespoons milk
- TOPPING:
- 2 egg whites
- 1/2 cup sugar
- 2 cups unsweetened raspberries

Instructions

In a large bowl, mix flour, sugar, baking powder and salt. Mix well, then add butter, egg, and milk and stir in flour until a dough forms. Press dough into sides and bottom of greased 9-in. Pie plate and set aside.

Beat the egg whites until soft peaks and slowly add sugar a tablespoon-at-a-time until soft peaks get stiff, then add raspberries and top over crust.

Cook for 30-35 minutes a 350 degrees F until well

browned and cool on wire rack. You can refrigerate leftovers.

Blackberry and Blueberry Pie

Ingredients

- 2/3 cup shortening
- 2 cups all-purpose flour
- 1 teaspoon salt
- 5 tablespoons cold water
- 3/4 cup white sugar
- 1/3 cup all-purpose flour
- 1/2 teaspoon ground cinnamon
- 4 cups fresh blueberries
- 1 1/2 cups fresh blackberries
- 1 tablespoon lemon juice
- 2 tablespoons butter

Instructions

Cut the shortening into the 2 cups2 cups flour and salt it until the salt particles are almost small pea size. Moisten the flour with 1 Tbs. at a time of water and form into a large ball, rolling out onto a board. Make two rounds with dough and add 1 crust in 9" pie dish.

In a large bowl, mix sugar, flour, and cinnamon, then add berries. Place the filling in the crust lined pan and sprinkle with lemon juice. Add the 2nd top crust and cut slits in the top, seal and flute.

Bake for 35 to 45 minutes and cover edges with foil, removing foil the last 12 minutes of baking time.

Marshmallow Crissie Bars

Ingredients

- 3 tablespoons butter
- 1 teaspoon vanilla extract
- 4 cups miniature marshmallows
- 4 cups crisp rice cereal

Instructions

Grease a 9" x 13" pan with margarine or oil.

On low heat, melt the butter or margarine and add vanilla.

Melt marshmallows in butter constantly stirring then when marshmallows are melted, add cereal and stir to coat.

Place in the greased pan and press down evenly into pan with a sheet of wax paper.

Set for 2 – 3 hours and then cut into squares.

Summertime Strawberry Punch

Ingredients

- 1 (12 fluid ounce) can frozen pink lemonade concentrate, thawed, undiluted
- 2 (10 ounce) packages frozen unsweetened strawberries, partially thawed
- 1/4 cup sugar
- 2 cups cold strong brewed tea
- 2 liters ginger ale, chilled
- ice cubes

Instructions

Mix the drink concentrate strawberries and sugar in a blender or food processor and process until smooth with cover on. Pour in a large pitcher or punch bowl for serving and stir in the tea. Stir in the soda and ice and serve.

Peach Cake Dessert

Ingredients

- 1 cup sugar
- 1 tablespoon all-purpose flour
- 1 teaspoon ground cinnamon
- 5 medium fresh peaches, peeled and sliced

CAKE:

- 1/4 cup butter or margarine, softened
- 1/2 cup sugar
- 1 egg
- 1 cup all-purpose flour
- 2 teaspoons baking powder
- 1/4 teaspoon salt
- 1/4 cup milk

Instructions

Mix the flour, sugar and cinnamon in a bowl and add the peaches and toss to coat with sugary mixture. Place in a greased square baking pan and set aside. In a small mixing bowlmixing bowl, blend the butter and sugar together and add the beaten egg. Mix well and combine flour, salt, and baking powder and add to the creamed mixture alternating with ¼ cup milk. Drop onto the peaches covering over evenly and bake for 40 - 45 minutes or until tested clean. Serve warm.

Sweet Floret Salad

Ingredients

- 1/2 cup mayonnaise
- 1/3 cup sugar
- 1/4 cup vegetable oil
- 1/4 cup vinegar
- 1 medium head cauliflower, broken into florets
- 1 3/4 pounds fresh broccoli florets
- 1 medium red onion, sliced
- 1 medium yellow bell pepper, cut into 1" pieces (optional)
- 1/2 pound sliced bacon, cooked and crumbled

Instructions

Bring the following to a boil in a small saucepan: mayonnaise, sugar, oil and vinegar.

CConstantly whisk mixture and then remove and cool to room temperature.

Combine the remaining ingredients in a large bowl and toss with dressing. Cover and chill for a few hours, take out occasionally to stir.

Sunny Orange Lemonade

Ingredients

- 4 1/4 cups water, divided
- 1 cup sugar
- 3/4 cup lemon juice
- 3/4 cup orange juice
- 2 teaspoons grated lemon peel
- 1 teaspoon grated orange peel
- ice cubes
- Lemon slices

Instructions

Bring 1 ¼ cups water and 1 cup sugar to a boil in a saucepan, reduce heat, and simmer for 10 minutes, then cool. Add to a pitcher with lemon and orange juices and their peels. Cover and chill 1 hour or more. Add the remaining water and serve over ice.

Thick 'n' Zesty Ribs

Ingredients

- 4 pounds pork baby back ribs, cut into serving size pieces
- 1 teaspoon garlic salt
- 1 cup ketchup
- 1/2 cup vinegar
- 1/4 cup sugar
- 1 1/2 teaspoons chili powder
- 1 teaspoon salt
- 1 teaspoon paprika
- 1 teaspoon ground mustard
- 1 teaspoon celery seed
- 1/2 teaspoon pepper

Instructions

Preheat oven to 350 degrees F and grease a 9 x 13 x 2 inch baking dish.

Add the ribs to prepared dish and massage with garlic salt.

Bake for 45 minutes and drain.

In a small bowl mix remaining ingredients and pour over the ribs return to bake for 40-50 minutes, while basting a few times during cook time. Cook until tender.

Raspberry Meringue Pie

Ingredients

- 1 cup all-purpose flour
- 1/3 cup sugar
- 1 teaspoon baking powder
- 1/4 teaspoon salt
- 2 tablespoons cold butter or margarine
- 1 egg, beaten
- 2 tablespoons milk
- TOPPING:
- 2 egg whites
- 1/2 cup sugar
- 2 cups unsweetened raspberries

Instructions

In a large bowl, mix flour, sugar, baking powder and salt. Mix well, then add butter, egg, and milk and stir in flour until a dough forms. Press dough into sides and bottom of greased 9-in. Pie plate and set aside.

Beat the egg whites until soft peaks and slowly add sugar a tablespoon-at-a-time until soft peaks get stiff, then add raspberries and top over crust.

Cook for 30-35 minutes a 350 degrees F until well browned and cool on wire rack. You can refrigerate leftovers.

Blackberry and Blueberry Pie

Ingredients

- 2/3 cup shortening
- 2 cups all-purpose flour
- 1 teaspoon salt
- 5 tablespoons cold water
- 3/4 cup white sugar
- 1/3 cup all-purpose flour
- 1/2 teaspoon ground cinnamon
- 4 cups fresh blueberries
- 1 1/2 cups fresh blackberries
- 1 tablespoon lemon juice
- 2 tablespoons butter

Instructions

Cut the shortening into the 2 cups2 cups flour and salt it until the salt particles are almost small pea size. Moisten the flour with 1 Tbs. at a time of water and form into a large ball, rolling out onto a board. Make two rounds with dough and add 1 crust in 9" pie dish.

In a large bowl, mix sugar, flour, and cinnamon, then add berries. Place the filling in the crust lined pan and sprinkle with lemon juice. Add the 2nd top crust and cut slits in the top, seal and flute.

Bake for 35 to 45 minutes and cover edges with foil, removing foil the last 12 minutes of baking time.

Marshmallow Crispie Bars

Ingredients

- 3 tablespoons butter
- 1 teaspoon vanilla extract
- 4 cups miniature marshmallows
- 4 cups crisp rice cereal

Instructions

Grease a 9 x 13 inch pan with cooking spray or butter.

Melt 3 Tbs. butter on low heat and add vanilla, melt marshmallows into butter and stir well.

Stir in the cereal when marshmallows have melted and stir to coat cereal.

Add to greased pan and press mixture down evenly with wax paper sheet.

Let it set for 2 hours or so and then cut into squares.

Best Brownies

Ingredients

- 1/2 cup butter
- 1 cup white sugar
- 2 eggs
- 1 teaspoon vanilla extract
- 1/3 cup unsweetened cocoa powder
- 1/2 cup all-purpose flour
- 1/4 teaspoon salt
- 1/4 teaspoon baking powder
- 3 tablespoons butter, softened
- 3 tablespoons unsweetened cocoa powder
- 1 tablespoon honey
- 1 teaspoon vanilla extract
- 1 cup confectioners' sugar

Instructions

Preheat oven to 350 degrees F and grease and lightly flour an 8 inch pan.

Melt ½ cup butter in saucepan and remove to add eggs, sugar, and 1 tsp. Vanilla. Mix well and beat in 1/3 cup cocoa, ½ cup flour, salt, and baking powder and transfer to the prepared baking pan.

Bake for 25 to 30 minutes, being careful not to overcook.

Make the frosting: Mix 3 Tbs butter, 3 Tbs. cocoa, 1
Tbs. honey, 1 tsp. Vanilla, and 1 cup confectioner's sugar.
Frost the brownies while warm.

Supa-Dupa Egg Sandwich

Ingredients

- 1/4 pound extra lean ground beef, formed into patties.
- 2 (1 ounce) slices bread
- ketchup
- mayonnaise
- 1 egg
- 2 slices mozzarella cheese
- 2 slices ham
- 1 slice fresh tomato

Instructions

On medium heat, place a frying pan and cook beef patties till done.

Fry an egg on medium heat, flip and cover with cheese, cook until yolk is hardened and cheese has melted.

Place some ketchup and mayo (or desired condiments) onto bread slices and add the egg on one slice of bread. Heat ham in the skillet and place on the egg when warm enough (I like my ham a little grilled). Top with hamburger patties and tomato slices and add the other slice of bread and cut in two.

Muesli Bars I

Ingredients

- 1/2 cup unsalted butter
- 1/3 cup packed brown sugar
- 3 tablespoons honey
- 1 cup quick cooking oats
- 1/3 cup chopped hazelnuts
- 1/3 cup shredded coconut
- 1/3 cup sesame seeds

Instructions

Preheat oven to 350 degrees F. and grease an 11 x 7 inch baking pan.

Mix the butter, brown sugar, and honey in a saucepan and cook until butter melts and sugar dissolves, remove and add remaining ingredients. Stir with a wooden spoon until flavors are well meshed. Press into baking pan and cook 15 to 18 minutes until top is golden brown, then let cool and cut into bars.

4th Of July Beans

Ingredients

- 1 lb. lean ground beef, browned and drained
- 1 pkg. onion soup (Lipton)
- 1/2 c. water
- 2 (1 lb. 12 oz.) cans B & M beans
- 1 c. ketchup
- 2 tbsp. mustard
- 2 tsp. vinegar
- 2 tbsp. brown sugar
- Partially cooked bacon (optional)

Instructions

In a large saucepan, brown the beef and when done, add all ingredients and top with the bacon. Transfer to a baking dish and cook for 20 minutes at 400 degrees F.

4th Of July Punch

Ingredients

- 4 c. cranberry juice
- 4 c. pineapple juice
- 2 qt. ginger ale
- 1 1/2 c. sugar
- 1 tbsp. almond extract

Instructions

Mix all ingredients in a large punch bowl and stir, until sugar dissolves. You can serve with a molded ice ring if you like.

July 4th Dandy

Ingredients

- 1/4 c. salted peanuts, chopped
- 4 lg. bananas
- 4 1/2 oz. frozen whipped topping, thawed
- 12 maraschino cherries
- Knife
- Scissors
- Bowl
- Tablespoon n
- Cutting board
- Toothpick flags

Instructions

Slice bananas lengthwise and cut away ½ inch of peel along slits, emptying into a bowl. Scoop fruit out carefully and save peels.

Blend whipped topping with bananas pieces and fill each banana with mixture then top with nuts then cherries and decorate with toothpick flags.

4th Of July Beans

Ingredients

- 8 strips bacon
- 4 onions, sliced thin
- 2 (28 oz.) cans baked beans
- 1 (16 oz.) can butter beans, drained
- 1 (16 oz.) can pinto beans, drained
- 1 (16 oz.) can Lima beans, drained

SAUCE:

- 1/2 c. vinegar
- 1 tsp. garlic salt
- 1 tsp. salt
- 1 tsp. dry mustard
- 1/2 c. brown sugar

Instructions

Fry the bacon ½ way through and remove from pan to saute onions until tender and soft, drain and place the beans in a casserole dish.

Mix the sauce ingredients and simmer for 3 minutes.

Mix with beans in dish and bake for 1 hour at 350 degrees.

4th Of July Salad Or Salad Bars

Ingredients

- 2 pkg. Pillsbury crescent rolls
- 12 oz. cream cheese
- 3/4 c. salad dressing (Miracle Whip)
- 1 tsp. garlic salt
- 1 tsp. dill weed
- Small bits of broccoli, onion, tiny carrots, sliced, radishes, sliced,
- Celery and cauliflower

Instructions

Press the rolls into jelly roll pan and bake for 10 minutes at 350 degrees F. Cool completely and mix all ingredients in a bowl, spreading over baked rolls and place the veggies on top, serve.

July 4th Snacks

Ingredients

- 1 pkg. (4 serving size) Jello brand berry blue flavored gelatin
- 1 pkg. (4 serving size) Jello brand gelatin, any red flavor
- 2 c. boiling water
- 1 c. cold water
- 2 c. Cool Whip

Instructions

In two bowls, Make the Jell-O as directed and stir in ½ cup cold water into gelatin, transfer to two 8 inch square pans and chill 3 hours. Cut up each pan in ½ inch cubes when set and spoon blue cubes into 8 dessert cups cover with whipped topping and top with red cubes the same way.

4th Of July Bread

Ingredients

- 1 loaf French bread
- 1/2 c. softened butter
- 1 c. green chilies
- 1/2 c. mayonnaise
- 1/4 lb. Monterey Jack cheese

Instructions

Cut the bread in triangles and spread butter on top with green chilies on top of butter. Add mayo and cheese to top of chilies and butter and bake in oven at 350 degrees for 20 minutes.

Can be frozen as well.

"4th Of July Salad"

Ingredients

- 1 container of cool whip, thawed
- 1 can cherry pie filling
- 1 can crushed pineapple, drained
- 1 can Eagle Brand milk (condensed)

Combine all ingredients in large bowl. Let chill for 2 hours

- 1 baked angel food cake
- 1 pt. heavy cream
- 1/2 c. sugar
- 1 tsp. vanilla
- 1 1/2 c. blueberries
- 1 1/4 c. sliced strawberries

Instructions

Slice the cake in 3 separate layers. Whisk the whipped cream and add vanilla and sugar until it thickens. Make the layers with cream and alternating slices of cake. On the top of 1st layer, add ¾ cup blueberries then on the 2nd layer, ¾ cup sliced strawberries. Add top layer and frost cake with whipped topping mixture adding a few berries for decoration and chill to serve.

4th Of July Salad

Ingredients

- 1 pkg. (3 oz.) raspberry Jello
- 3 c. hot water
- 1 env. Knox gelatin
- 1 c. sugar
- 1 c. milk
- 1 tsp. vanilla
- 1 (8 oz.) cream cheese, softened
- 1/2 c. cold water
- 1/2 c. nuts, chopped (pecans)
- 16 oz. can blueberries (& juice)

Instructions

1st Layer: In 2 cups hot water, dissolve Jell-O in 8 or 9 inch pan and chill in fridge to set.

2nd Layer: Add ½ cup cold water to plain gelatin in bowl. Heat milk and sugar in a small saucepan and add the gelatin/water mix. Stirring slowly, add vanilla, cream cheese and nuts. Spread over the first layer and set in fridge.

3rd Layer: In hot water in a bowl , dissolve 1 package of Jell-O and stir in the blueberries and juice, cool and transfer to pan as third layer.

Make sure each layer is well set before adding the next layer.

4th Of July Cake

Ingredients

- 1 pkg. Duncan Hines fudge marble cake mix
- pkg. strawberry Jello
- 3/4 c. boiling water
- 1/2 c. cold water
- 1 tub vanilla frosting
- 4 oz. cream cheese, softened
- tsp. lemon juice
- 20 fresh strawberries

Instructions

In a small bowl, dissolve gelatin in boiling water and add the cold water and set aside.

Make cake as directed and cool for 30 minutes in pan. Poke deep holes in cake 1" apart and pour the Jell-O over cake, filling the holes. Place in refrigerator and make frosting.

Combine lemon juice and cream cheese until blended, then add vanilla frosting and spread over cake. You can decorate with th fruit if you like.

Cake must be kept in fridge and served cold.

4th Of July Salad

Ingredients

- 1 pkg. raspberry Jello
- 1 pkg. blackberry Jello
- 1 env. unflavored gelatin
- 1 c. half & half
- 1 c. sugar
- 1 tsp. vanilla
- 1 (8 oz.) pkg. cream cheese, room temp.
- 1/2 c. chopped nuts (any)
- 1 c. whole blueberries (fresh or frozen)
- 1 c. strawberries (fresh or frozen)
- 1 (8"x12") pan or 2 (5 cup) molds

Instructions

In 1 ½ cups boiling water, dissolve Jell-O and add the strawberries, pour into a pan and chill in fridge to firm.

In ½ cup boiling water, soften the unflavored gelatin. In a small saucepan on low heat, combine half 'n half with sugar until hot but not boiling. Add the gelatin, vanilla and cream cheese (also nuts if using) slowly and use an electric mixer to break up cheese into smaller pieces and chill in fridge.

Dissolve the blackberry Jell-O in 1 ½ v cups boiling water and add the whole blueberries return to fridge to set.

4th Of July Sirloin

2 lb. sirloin

MARINADE:

- 1/2 c. soy sauce
- 1/2 c. dry red wine
- 1 tbsp. fresh minced ginger
- 1 tbsp. minced garlic
- 2 tbsp. chopped cilantro
- Freshly ground black pepper

Instructions

In a bowl, add all marinade ingredients and mix well. Cut up the meat into chunks and add to bowl tossing to coat, cover and chill overnight in fridge.

Can be cooked on coals or 4 inches from the heat. Broil each side 3- 4 minutes and brush with marinade.

4th Of July Sloppy Joes

Ingredients

- 1 bunch celery, chopped
- 1 med. onion, chopped
- 2 tbsp. butter
- 2 tbsp. vinegar
- 2 tbsp. brown sugar
- 4 tbsp. lemon juice
- 1 c. catchup
- 1/2 tsp. chopped parsley
- 1/2 tbsp. prepared mustard
- 1/2 c. water
- 3 tbsp. Worcestershire sauce
- Salt and pepper to taste
- Small can of tomato sauce
- 1/2 tsp. Tabasco sauce
- Quart tomatoes
- 8 to 10 lbs. ground beef

Instructions

In a large skillet, brown the onion and celery with butter and mix in the ground beef when celery is tender. Brown meat and add the remaining ingredients, simmer a few hours.

4th Of July Macaroni Salad

Ingredients

- 1 pkg. shell macaroni (cooked)
- 1 med. green pepper, chopped
- 1 can pimiento, chopped
- 1 med. onion, chopped
- 1 c. sweet pickles, chopped
- 1/2 c. celery, chopped
- 1/2 c. mayonnaise
- 1 tbsp. vinegar
- 1/4 c. sugar
- Salt and pepper to taste

Instructions

In a large bowl, mix all ingredients and set for 2-3 hours or overnight to allow flavors to integrate.

4th Of July Vanilla Ice Cream

Ingredients

- 1 c. sugar
- 1 tbsp. flour
- 1/4 tsp. salt
- 3 egg yolks, slightly beaten
- 2 c. cream
- 2 tsp. vanilla

Instructions

In a small saucepan on low heat, scald the milk and mix with sugar, flour, and salt mixing well. Slowly adding and cooking on direct heat 5 minutes.

Remove and stir 3 tbsp. mixture into egg yolks very fast aAnd add the rest, return to heat and cook for 10 minutes until mixture coats a spoon. Remove to cool.

Add the vanilla and cream and chill in fridge.

4th Of July Molded Salad

Ingredients

- 12 c. oiled mold
- 16 oz. fresh strawberries
- 1 1/2 c. boiling water
- 1 1/2 c. cream cheese
- 2 tbsp. whipping cream
- 1 1/2 c. boiling water
- 16 oz. drained canned blueberries
- 3/4 c. blueberry syrup

Instructions

Mix the cream cheese and whipping cream until smooth in a small bowl.

In another bowl, combine boiling water with canned blueberries and syrup until smooth.

Line the bottom of mold with 1 ½ cup boiling water.

Combine all and add strawberry mixture to bottom of mold and chill for 45 minutes. Add to cream cheese mixture and return to fridge to chill for another 45 minutes, then add the blueberry mixture and chill 1 more hour, unmold and serve on top of lettuce pieces.

Barbecued Creamed Potatoes (4th Of July)

Ingredients

- 3 tbsp. flour
- 3 tbsp. butter
- 2 c. milk
- 1/4 tsp. Tabasco sauce
- 1 1/2 tsp. salt
- 2 tsp. chopped parsley
- 2 tsp. chopped pimento
- 4 c. potatoes, cooked and diced
- Cracker Barrel sharp cheese
- Paprika

Instructions

In a skillet, make the paste with flour and butter, stirring until smooth. Add milk and boil, then remove from heat and add seasonings. Mix in the potatoes and transfer to a baking dish, top with lots of cheese and paprika and bake for 30 minutes at 400 degrees.

Corned Beef Special (4th Of July)

Ingredients

- 2 lg. onions, finely chopped
- 2 tbsp. bacon grease
- 1 can corned beef, broken into pieces
- 1 lg. can tomatoes
- Salt and pepper to taste

Instructions

Saute the onions in bacon grease but do not brown. Stir in the tomatoes and corned beef and mix well.

Simmer mixture and stir until almost all of the liquid is gone. Season with salt and pepper.

4th Of July Pie

Ingredients

- 1 pkg. sugar cookie dough or prepared graham cracker crust
- 1/2 c. sugar
- 3 tbsp. cornstarch
- 1 1/2 c. orange juice
- 3 c. fresh strawberries, halved
- 3 c. fresh blueberries
- 1/4 c. lemon juice

Instructions

Preheat oven to 400 degrees F. Press the prepared dough in a 9" pie pan and bake for 8 minutes, then cool.

Stir together sugar and cornstarch in a saucepan and add the orange juice until it becomes a smooth mixture. On medium heat, bring to a boil for one minute then remove and add lemon juice.

In a small bowl, mix ½ this juice with blueberries, and in another, ½ juice with strawberries.

Add strawberries to outside of crust and blueberries inside. Chill for 4 hours and serve with whipped cream.

Hot Dog Sauce (4th Of July)

Ingredients

- 1 tbsp. brown sugar
- 1/4 tsp. paprika
- 2 tbsp. lemon juice or vinegar
- 1 lg. chopped onion
- 1/4 green pepper, chopped
- 3 lb. ground beef
- 1/2 c. oil
- 1 lg. can tomato sauce
- 1 c. catchup or chili sauce
- 4 tbsp. Worcestershire sauce
- 1 tbsp. chili powder
- 1 tsp. hot sauce
- 1 tsp. salt
- 1/4 tsp. pepper
- 2 tbsp. mustard seed

Instructions

In a skillet, saute beef with the onion and pepper until browned and veggies are soft. Mix in the remaining ingredients and simmer for 45 minutes to an hour

4th Of July Pie

Ingredients

- 3 oz. pkg. lemon gelatin
- 2/3 c. boiling water
- 2 c. ice cubes
- 8 oz. container frozen whipped topping, thawed
- 1/2 c. whole fresh blueberries
- 1/2 c. sliced fresh strawberries
- 9 inch graham cracker crust

Instructions

Dissolve the gelatin in boiling water for 2 minutes while stirring. Add the ice cubes and stir 2-3 minutes until this thickens. Take out any melted ice and blend in the whipped topping until it gets smooth. Add the fruit and chill to firm. Turn onto a pie shell and return to fridge to chill 2 hours.

Independence Day Cake (4th Of July)

Ingredients

- 1/4 tsp. salt
- 1 c. sugar
- 1 stick butter
- 2 egg yolks
- 1/4 tsp. orange extract
- 1/2 tsp. lemon extract
- 1 1/2 c. cake flour
- 1 1/2 tsp. baking powder
- 1/2 c. milk

Instructions

Preheat oven to 350 degrees. Blend the salt, sugar, and butter and add the yolks, beating in until fluffy. Stir in the extracts and sift flour and baking powder. Beat the egg whites till they are stiff, then fold into the batter. Place in a 9-inch square pan and bake for 40 minutes.

Mexican Independence Day Tamale Pie

Ingredients

- 1 lb. ground beef
- 1 1/2 tsp. garlic powder
- 1 (7 1/2 oz.) can Rosario refried beans, any variety
- 1 (16 oz.) jar Rosario mild chunky Picayune sauce or chunky salsa dip
- 1 (8 3/4 oz.) can whole kernel corn, drained
- 1/2 c. sliced green onions
- 1/4 c. chopped cilantro
- 1/4 tsp. ground cumin
- 1 (15-16 oz.) pkg. cornbread mix, prepared according to pkg.
- 1 c. shredded Cheddar cheese

Instructions

Brown the meat with garlic powder and drain well. Add remaining ingredients to a large bowl with meat except cornbread mix and the cheese. Place mixture into the bottom of a 13 x 9 x 2 baking dish. In a small bowl add the cheese and cornbread mix and spread over meat mixture.

Bake for 30 – 35 minutes until it the toothpick tests done.
Cool 10 – 15 minutes and serve.

Berries Independence Day

Ingredients

- 1 qt. ripe strawberries, hulled
- 1/2 c. currant jelly
- 1/4 c. apricot preserves
- 1 pt. blueberries
- 1 pt. sour cream
- Pound cake

Instructions

Cut the larger strawberries into halves. Whisk the jelly until smooth in a bowl, adding the fruit and mixing to coat with mixture. Place this in a bowl and add the blueberries, tossing to coat.

Transfer blueberries to center of serving platter and add the sour cream, smoothing it and making a circle around the berries. Make another border with strawberries around the sour cream and place slices of pound cake on a plate to serve.

French-American Potato Salad

Ingredients

- 3 tablespoons best quality red wine vinegar
- Fine sea salt
- 1/2 cup extra virgin olive oil
- 2 cloves garlic, finely minced
- 2 pounds new potatoes
- 1 small red onion, very thinly sliced
- 3/4 of a cup of cornices (tiny French pickles), cut in thin rounds
- 1 bunch radishes, cut in small rounds
- 1/4 cup capers
- 4 large, hard-cooked eggs, diced

Instructions

Whisk wine with salt in large bowl and add the olive oil and garlic.

Steam potatoes 20 minutes until tender. Remove from steamer and cool enough to peel and cut them into thick rounds. Add to vinaigrette and toss then let sit to cool completely.

Stir in the remaining ingredients and toss well, seasoning to taste with salt and pepper. Set for 2 hours allowing flavors to mesh.

ALL RIGHTS RESERVED. No part of this publication may be reproduced or transmitted in any form whatsoever, electronic, or mechanical, including photocopying, recording, or by any informational storage or retrieval system without express written, dated and signed permission from the author.

DISCLAIMER AND/OR LEGAL NOTICES: Every effort has been made to accurately represent this book and it's potential. Results vary with every individual, and your results may or may not be different from those depicted. No promises, guarantees or warranties, whether stated or implied, have been made that you will produce any specific result from this book. Your efforts are individual and unique, and may vary from those shown. Your success depends on your efforts, background and motivation.

The material in this publication is provided for educational and informational purposes only and is not intended as medical advice. The information contained in this book should not be used to diagnose or treat any illness, metabolic disorder, disease or health problem. Always consult your physician or health care provider before beginning any nutrition or exercise program. Use of the programs, advice, and information contained in this book is at the sole choice and risk of the readers.

Made in United States
Troutdale, OR
05/30/2024

20228285R00076